# Lecture Notes in Operations Research and Mathematical Systems

Economics, Computer Science, Information and Control

Edited by M. Beckmann, Providence and H. P. Künzi, Zürich

Series: Lehrstuhl für Betriebswirtschaftslehre, Universität Mainz. Adviser: H. Müller-Merbach

## 37

## H. Müller-Merbach
Lehrstuhl für Betriebswirtschaftslehre
Johannes-Gutenberg-Universität, Mainz

## On Round-Off Errors in Linear Programming

Springer-Verlag
Berlin · Heidelberg · New York 1970

Advisory Board

H. Albach · A. V. Balakrishnan · F. Ferschl
W. Krelle · N. Wirth

This work is subject to copyright. All rights are reserved, whether the whole or part of the material is concerned, specifically those of translation, reprinting, re-use of illustrations, broadcasting, reproduction by photocopying machine or similar means, and storage in data banks.

Under § 54 of the German Copyright Law where copies are made for other than private use, a fee is payable to the publisher, the amount of the fee to be determined by agreement with the publisher.

© by Springer-Verlag Berlin · Heidelberg 1970. Library of Congress Catalog Card Number 76-137141 Printed in Germany. Title No. 3786

## Preface

This report is a slightly revised version of a mimeographed paper written 1963/64 at the Operations Research Center of the University of California. Due to the many who asked for a copy of that paper, which is out of stock, I decided to publish this new edition of it.

There are many publications on round-off errors in general (e.g. [8], [9], [13]), but very few on round-off errors in linear programming. According to Philip Wolfe [14] in 1965 this was the first one: "It is correct, to a close approximation, to say that there is no theory of error in the solution of linear programming problems. We know of only one recorded study of the subject .. which ... mainly reports observations made in the course of solving actual problems."

This investigation was my first attempt to learn about the cumulation of round-off errors in linear programming procedures. No claim is made that the results summarized in this paper offer a proper answer to every question dealing with recognizing, measuring, eliminating, and avoiding round-off errors. Many interesting problems still remain uninvestigated and unsolved.

Mainz, July 1970                                    Heiner Müller-Merbach

Contents

    I. Introduction .......................................... 1

   II. The Examples ......................................... 3

  III. The Programs ........................................ 7

   IV. The Increase and Cumulation of Round-Off Errors ...... 11

    V. The Use of Easily Computed Checks as a Trigger for
       Error Elimination ................................... 14

   VI. The Zero-Check for Eliminating Non-Significant
       Elements ............................................ 17

  VII. "Ill-Conditioned" Vertices ........................... 26

 VIII. Some General Remarks ................................. 30

   IX. Acknowledgment ....................................... 34

Appendix ................................................... 35

References ................................................. 47

# I. Introduction

Due to the limited number of digits or bits per storage location in electronic computers, round-off errors arise during arithmetic operations. Depending upon the kind of operation, the structure of the data, and the skillfulness of the program, these errors increase and spread out more or less quickly during a continued computation process in which the computed data affected by errors are themselves used for generating new data.

The purpose of this investigation was to learn about the increase of round-off errors in linear programming procedures. Less attention was paid to the theory of round-off errors or to the effectiveness of error elimination procedures. In regard to these questions the results of investigations which have been made on round-off errors in a more general context dealing with matrix inversion and eigenvalue problems could be used for the purposes of this paper.

The emphasis of this investigation lay rather on studying the behavior of typical linear programming problems from the point of view of error cumulation. Five questions were of particular interest:

(1) How fast do the mean relative round-off errors increase during the linear programming iterations and of what size are the maximal relative errors?

(2) Is there a good correlation between the average error (or the maximal error) and any easily calculated check?

(3) What are the effects of setting those elements of the coefficient matrix equal to zero which obviously consist only of round-off errors? In particular, (a) the effect on the average error, (b) the effect on the number of non-zero elements, and (c) the effect on the number of numerical operations in the succeeding iterations were studied.

(4) How efficient are reiteration techniques (cleaning-up techniques) for eliminating the errors, how often are they to be used, and do the checks mentioned in point (2) serve as a suitable trigger for starting error elimination?

(5) How does an "ill-conditioned" vertex accelerate the growth of round-

off errors; and how can pivoting at "ill-conditioned" vertices be avoided?

The investigations have been carried out with 14 test problems. Most of these problems were selected from the SCEMP-project (Standardized Computational Experiments in Mathematical Programming, see [1]) and from some other practical problems. Besides these, some random number problems were generated which, however, behaved too well; i. e., were not significant as far as round-off errors are concerned.

Three different linear programming codes were programmed for this investigation:

Program 1: The normal simplex method.

Program 2: The revised simplex method with explicit form of the inverse.

Program 3: The symmetric revised simplex method (see [6], [7] pp. 218-224), a method with a modified product form of the inverse.

All these codes were written in FORTRAN II for the IBM 7o9o computer. As a predecessor, a normal simplex method code written in ALGOL for the computer NCR 8o3 B was used for making the first numerical experiments.

The codes were programmed for the special purpose of this investigation. A lot of checks, counts, and bookkeeping and statistical devices, and additional outputs were inserted which made the programs inefficient from the point of view of solving a linear programming problem rapidly.

## II. The Examples

Before mentioning some details of the test problems, several general remarks on the notation used in the following chapters must be made.

The linear programming problem is stated by:

Maximize the objective function

$$\sum_{j=1}^{n} c_j x_j = z \tag{1}$$

subject to the constraints

$$\sum_{j=1}^{n} a_{ij} x_j \leq b_i \qquad i=1,\ldots,m \tag{2}$$

and to the lower bounds

$$x_j \geq 0 \qquad j=1,\ldots,n \tag{3}$$

By adding slack variables to the constraints the inequalities (2) can be reset by the equations:

$$\sum_{j=1}^{n} a_{ij} x_j + x_{n+i} = b_i \qquad i=1,\ldots,m \tag{4}$$

and the additional lower bounds

$$x_{n+i} \geq 0 \tag{5}$$

The size of this system is m times n. It has m constraints and therefore at any state of solution m basic variables and n non-basic variables. The starting set of basic variables is given by the m slack variables $x_{n+i}$ while the $x_j$ (j=1,...,n) are the non-basic variables.

For negative right hands $b_i$ the requirement (5) is not fulfilled, and the current solution is not feasible. In this case a second objective function of the kind:

$$\text{Maximize} \sum_{j=1}^{n} c'_j x_j = z' \tag{6}$$

with $c_j' = -\sum_{\substack{i=1 \\ b_i<0}}^{m} a_{ij}$  (7)

instead of equation (1) serves for the purpose of finding a first feasible solution (phase 1).

Some of the test problems contained constraints of the type:

$$\sum_{j=1}^{n} a_{ij}x_j = b_i \qquad (8)$$

instead of the inequalities (2). In these cases the problems were transformed into (2) by pivoting once in each of those equations. By this procedure the number n of non-basic variables was decreased by the number of equations of type (8). This preparation of the data was carried out by means of a special program.

The optimal solution of a linear program consisting of the system of equations (1), (4), (3), (5), and possibly (6) is found after several iterations or pivot steps. Pivoting means the exchange of one non-basic variable for a basic variable. In the codes used in this investigation the pivot column s (the non-basic variable which enters the basis) is that one which has the largest positive coefficient in the objective function (1) or (6), respectively. As pivot row r (the basic variable which drops out of the basis) that row is selected which has the smallest positive ratio of the right hand side element to the element of the pivot column.

The main operation in each of the codes is of the type:

$$a_{ij}^* = a_{ij} - \frac{a_{is}a_{rj}}{a_{rs}} \qquad (9)$$

where the asterisk indicates the new element. In FORTRAN [+)] this procedure looks like:

$$A(I,J) = A(I,J) - PC(I)*PR(J) \qquad (1o)$$

---

[+)] The short FORTRAN statements mentioned in this paper shall only illustrate the procedure and outline the idea behind it. For the purpose of simplifying the explanation, the computational details for saving operation time are not considered here.

where PC(I) stand for the elements $a_{is}$ of the (old) pivot column and PR(J) stands for the elements $\frac{a_{rj}}{a_{rs}}$ of the (new) pivot row.

At least as many iterations have to be carried out as non-basic variables of the starting solution are basic variables in the optimal solution. Usually, the number of iterations is much higher since the variables of the optimal solution are not known in advance.

The main test problems are summarized in Table 1. The columns of the table have the following meaning:

Col. 1    Number of the problem. The first eight problems were taken from the SCEMP project (Compare with [1]; partly modified by eliminating figures like equation (8)); problems 9 - 11 are also practical problems; problem 12 - 14 are generated by random numbers.

Col. 2    Original number in the SCEMP project.

Col. 3    Number m of constraints of type (2).

Col. 4    Number n of non-basic variables.

Col. 5    Number q of non-zero elements $a_{ij}$ in the initial matrix.

Col. 6    Percentage $\frac{q}{m.n}$ of non-zero elements in the initial matrix.

Col. 7    Number of negative $b_i$ (Infeasibility of the starting solution).

Col. 8    Number of $b_i = 0$ in the starting solution.

Col. 9    Number of non-basic variables of the starting solution which become basic variables in the optimal solution (Minimum number of iterations). In the case of several optimal solutions, the smallest number recorded is given.

| 1 | 2 | 3 | 4 | 5 | 6 $\frac{q}{m \cdot n}$ (%) | 7 No. of $b_i < 0$ | 8 No. of $b_i = 0$ | 9 Min. No. of |
|---|---|---|---|---|---|---|---|---|
| Number | SCEMP Number | m | n | q | | | | Iterations |
| 1 | 1C | 5 | 9 | 38 | 84.5 | 5 | 0 | 5 |
| 2 | 3B | 17 | 10 | 46 | 27.0 | 3 | 3 | 7 |
| 3 | 1D | 27 | 18 | 198 | 40.7 | 19 | 0 | 12 |
| 4 | 1A | 33 | 31 | 191 | 18.6 | 11 | 0 | 13 |
| 5 | 5A | 34 | 44 | 313 | 20.9 | 0 | 27 | 18 |
| 6 | 1G | 48 | 52 | 340 | 13.6 | 7 | 6 | 35 |
| 7 | 2A | 30 | 73 | 690 | 31.5 | 0 | 22 | 16 |
| 8 | 1E | 31 | 75 | 843 | 36.2 | 2 | 10 | 16 |
| 9 | - | 16 | 14 | 136 | 60.6 | 0 | 6 | 4 |
| 10 | - | 16 | 14 | 136 | 60.6 | 0 | 6 | 7 |
| 11 | - | 17 | 14 | 150 | 63.0 | 1 | 6 | 7 |
| 12 | - | 20 | 20 | 85 | 21.3 | 0 | 0 | 11 |
| 13 | - | 10 | 40 | 98 | 24.5 | 0 | 0 | 10 |
| 14 | - | 30 | 50 | 149 | 9.9 | 0 | 0 | 21 |

Table 1: Sample of test problems

Some other small problems (taken from the literature) were also evaluated, but the results are not as interesting as the results of these larger problems.

Furthermore, some small arbitrarily constructed problems were used for studying the behavior at "ill-conditioned" vertices. These are corners of the polyhedron formed by the constraints where two or more hyperplanes intersect at a very slight angle.

## III. The Programs

As mentioned above, three different codes of the simplex method were used. In each of them the number of operations of the type described by equation (9) was counted. Furthermore, the number of non-zero elements of the "working coefficient matrix" was recorded. By "working coefficient matrix" shall be understood:

(1) The current m x n coefficient matrix in the normal simplex method (Program 1),

(2) The current inverse (in explicit form) of the basis, (including the right hand side vector and the vector of the simplex multipliers) in program 2,

(3) The current inverse (in symmetric product form; no reinversion) of the basis in program 3.

Each of the programs contained a device for setting those coefficients equal to zero which obviously (or with nearly 100% probability) consist only of round-off errors. If $|a^*_{ij}| \leq \epsilon |a_{ij}|$ with $\epsilon \ll 1$ after computing equation (9), it can be assumed that actually $a^*_{ij}$ should be equal to zero. The check values $\epsilon = 10^{-4}$, $\epsilon = 10^{-5}$, and $\epsilon = 10^{-6}$ were used. In the case of $|a^*_{ij}|$ being smaller than $\epsilon |a_{ij}|$, it has been set equal to zero. This is to be justified by the assumption that the precision of the initial input data is not higher than $\log \frac{1}{\epsilon}$ digits. The number of the elements vanishing after this "zero check" as well as the logarithmic mean value of their ratio $|\frac{a^*_{ij}}{a_{ij}}|$ and the largest element among them were recorded.

Each of the three programs contained some check computations for easy estimation of the average round-off error. For instance, one check in program 1 was based upon a column vector containing the sums of the coefficients of each row and a row vector containing the sums of the coefficients of each column. These two vectors were handled like vectors of the coefficient matrix. Now, the elements of this column vector have to add up to the same value as the row vector sum. The relative difference between the sums might give some estimate of the average precision of the working coefficient matrix. Details of this point will be discussed in Chapter V.

The main additional insertion to programs 1 and 2 was a "reiteration" procedure for measuring (and optional elimination of) the round-off errors.

This technique is well-known for matrix inversions (see [1o], [11], [12], [13], [15]). Consider A to be a quadratic non-singular matrix and $A^{-1}$ the precise inverse of it. The computed inverse is called $A_c^{-1}$ which differs from $A^{-1}$ by round-off errors. By multiplying A by $A_c^{-1}$ and subtracting the unity matrix I the first error matrix $\Delta$ will be obtained:

$$\Delta = AA_c^{-1} - I \tag{11}$$

This computation of $\Delta$ has to be carried out with double precision. Multiplying equation (11) by $A^{-1}$ leads to:

$$A^{-1}\Delta = A_c^{-1} - A^{-1}$$

or

$$A^{-1} = A_c^{-1} - A^{-1}\Delta$$

and as a good approximation for small errors:

$$A^{-1} \approx A_c^{-1} - A_c^{-1}\Delta \tag{12}$$

The multiplication $A_c^{-1}\Delta$ can be carried out with single precision. If the improvement is not satisfactory the whole process can be repeated by considering the approximated matrix $A^{-1}$ of equation (12) as the computed matrix $A_c^{-1}$. As a matter of fact, in almost all the test problems one application of this reiteration procedure led to the exact result.

In order to apply this technique to the programs 1 und 2 of the simplex method, it had to be modified slightly for handling the working coefficient matrices. In program 1 the whole m x n matrix had to be considered. In program 2, in order to save computation time, the error calculations were carried out only for the non-unity vectors of the working matrix; i. e., only for the columns which do not represent a slack variable $x_{n+i}$ in the basis.

These error calculations can also be applied just to measure the errors without eliminating them. In this study the relative errors were of particular interest. By calling $(a_c)_{ij}$ the elements of the matrix $A_c^{-1}$ and $(a_c\delta)_{ij}$ the elements of the matrix $A_c^{-1}\Delta$ the relative errors were calculated by

$$e_{ij} = \left| \frac{(a_c\delta)_{ij}}{(a_c)_{ij} - (a_c\delta)_{ij}} \right| \tag{13}$$

for $(a_c)_{ij} \neq 0$ and $(a_c)_{ij} - (a_c\delta)_{ij} \neq 0$ and $(a_c\delta)_{ij} \neq 0$

and 
$$1 + \varepsilon^* > \left| \frac{(a_c)_{ij} - (a_c\delta)_{ij}}{(a_c)_{ij}} \right| > \varepsilon^* \tag{14}$$

with e. g. $\varepsilon^* = 0.5$

For features which fail check (14) one can consider this particular $(a_c)_{ij}$ as actually being zero, since the relative error usually would not become larger in value than 50% of the actual value of the corresponding matrix element.

For w as the number of $e_{ij} > 0$ the logarithmic mean:

$$M = \sum_{i,j} \frac{\log e_{ij}}{w} \tag{15}$$

and the logarithmic standard deviation:

$$S = \sqrt{\frac{1}{w} \sum_{i,j} (\log e_{ij})^2 - M^2} \tag{16}$$

were computed. Furthermore, the maximal relative error

$$E_{max} = \max_{i,j} (\log e_{ij}) \tag{17}$$

was recorded. The reason for computing the logarithmic mean and standard deviation (instead of the arithmetic mean and standard deviation) was that the logarithm corresponds better to the number of significant digits (= total digits of a storage location of a computer minus the digits spoiled by errors) of the single coefficients.

This error measurement has been made after every $k^{th}$ iteration (usually, k = 1 for small and k = 5 for larger problems). In most of the runs the errors were measured, but no elements were adjusted. In some runs, however, the elements of the working coefficient matrix were corrected according to equation (12) or set equal to zero after having failed check (14).

A fourth program derived from program 1 was developed for the purpose of avoiding pivoting at "ill-conditioned" vertices. The details will be given in Chapter VII.

## IV. The Increase and Cumulation of Round-Off Errors

To give an impression of how fast round-off errors may increase even in a not really ill-conditioned case, a short numerical example shall be discussed before reporting the results of the computer runs. The problem is to compute

$$e = a - b.c$$
and
$$g = d - e.f$$

(which is similar to two succeeding operations of equation (9)). The numerical values of the parameters are given in the following table in which the numbers are presented in the usual way as well as in the floating point FORTRAN format with 8-digit mantissa and the exponent:

$$a = 21 = .21000000 \text{ E } 02$$
$$b = 6 = .60000000 \text{ E } 01$$
$$c = 10/3 = .33333333 \text{ E } 01$$
$$d = .15 = .15000000 \text{ E } 00$$
$$f = 1/7 = .14285714 \text{ E } 00$$

The intermediate and final results are shown in the next table, where the first column contains the computed results (with the significant digits underlined) and the second column gives the precise results:

| | Computed Result | Precise Result |
|---|---|---|
| b.c = | .19999998 E 02 | .20000000 E 02 |
| e = | .10000020 E 01 | .10000000 E 01 |
| e.f = | .14285742 E 00 | .14285714 E 00 |
| g = | .71425800 E-02 | .71428571 E-02 |

In g there are only four of eight significant digits left, while the last four digits are spoiled by cumulated errors. In computers with decimal arithmetic the errors will increase as they did in this example. In computers with binary arithmetic, like the IBM 7o9o, the errors will arise somewhat more slowly, but the cumulation of existing errors will be the same. This example serves to show how fast an error may spread out. In most practical cases the average error will spread out less rapidly, though.

In the computer runs on linear programming in this investigation, the round-off errors have been measured after every $k^{th}$ iteration as outlined in Chapter III. The records of these errors contained the logarithmic mean value M of the relative error, its logarithmic standard deviation S, and the maximal relative error $E_{max}$. Some further records on the mean value of the absolute errors were made, which, however, do not seem to be as interesting and significant.

The increase of round-off errors was rather similar in the various problems:

(1) The logarithmic mean of the relative errors increased slowly but not always steadily from about M = -8 in the beginning (which is corresponding to the maximal accuracy [+]) of single precision computation) up to about M = -6 after some 30 to 50 iterations. This means that the average precision after that many iterations was about five to six digits. Corresponding to this, the average loss of precision was two to three digits.

(2) The logarithmic standard deviation accompanying this mean value usually remained rather constantly at a value of S = ± 1 (corresponding to one digit) and seldom went below S = ± .05 or above S = ± 1.5. Only a very slight tendency to increase with the number of iterations was noticed.

(3) The maximal relative error $E_{max}$ did not show any clear tendency to increase. Rather, it bounced around uncontrollably between $E_{max}$ = -4 and $E_{max}$ = -6, sometimes increasing, sometimes decreasing. Sometimes it even reached $E_{max}$ = -3. This means that the reliable precision was only three to four significant digits. Even when the errors were eliminated after every iteration, the maximal round-off error in the very next iteration often reached values of $E_{max}$ = -4.

Fortunately, the relative errors of the right hand side vector were usually smaller than the average error and did not very often cut off more

---

[+]) The actual precision of floating point operations on the IBM 7090 is 26 bits which is corresponding to little more than eight decimal digits since $2^{26}$ = 134343728.

than two digits from the actual numbers so that the remaining precision
was six or at least five digits. On the other hand, the objective function
vectors unfortunately proved themselves to be much more sensitive to round-
off errors than the other coefficients of the working matrix. The reason
for this seems to be that the (absolute)largest member of the objective
function is used for selecting the pivot column while the (relative)
smallest member of the right hand side vector serves for selecting the
pivot row. Thus the relative error of the pivot column element of the objective function tends to spread out faster than the error of the pivot
row element of the right hand side vector.

The results of the computer runs are shown in the appendix. Group I of
the figures (Fig. I-1 to I-11) in the appendix concerns the increase of
the mean and maximal relative errors. The upper heavy line in the figures
shows the mean errors while the lower line represents the maximal errors,
plotted over the iterations (pivot steps). Some figures contain the less
interesting standard deviation in addition to these lines.

The other lines drawn in the same figures refer to some check values which
are discussed in the following chapter.

The indication of the values of $\varepsilon$ corresponds to the zero check as briefly
outlined in Chapter III and as more thoroughly described in Chapter VI.

In some of the runs, error elimination according to equation (12) and
check (14) took place after each error measurement, as indicated below
each figure.

Since the results of the various problems do not differ much from each
other, only some typical runs are covered by the figures.

## V. The Use of Easily Computed Checks as a Trigger for Error Elimination

Several checks have been inserted in the three main programs in order to learn about their correlation to the average relative error.

One group of checks in program 1 and 3 was based upon a column vector containing the sums of the coefficients of each row and a row vector containing the sums of the coefficients of each column of the initial coefficient matrix. These vectors were set up before starting the linear programming procedure. Afterwards, they were handled like an additional row and an additional column vector of the working matrix. However, they were not allowed to be chosen as pivot row or pivot column, nor was the error measuring technique applied to them. After each iteration the sum of the elements of this additional column (SUM1) and row (SUM2) were computed. In addition, a third number (SUM3) was calculated which had been set equal to SUM1 in the beginning, and then in each iteration it was altered by the product of the pivot row element of the old additional column and the pivot column element of the new additional row corresponding to equation (9). In case there are no round-off errors the three sums should be equal after each iteration. Due to the errors, however, they differ from each other. The following four check values dealing with the relative differences were recorded in each iteration:

$$\text{Check1} = \log \left| \frac{SUM1 - SUM3}{SUM3} \right|$$

$$\text{Check2} = \log \left| \frac{SUM2 - SUM3}{SUM3} \right|$$

$$\text{Check3} = \log \left| \frac{SUM1 \cdot SUM2 - SUM3^2}{SUM3^2} \right|$$

$$\text{Check4} = \log \left( \frac{|SUM1| + |SUM2|}{2 \cdot |SUM3|} - 1 \right)$$

In program 2 a right hand side vector check was inserted. The sum of the elements of the right hand side vector after each iteration (SUM4) was compared with SUM5 which was set equal to the sum of the elements of the initial right hand side in the beginning and was then altered in each iteration by the product of the pivot row element of the right hand side vector and the sum of the elements of the pivot column. The check value due to their relative difference was:

$$\text{Check5} = \log \left| \frac{SUM5 - SUM4}{SUM4} \right|$$

All these check values were more or less related to the average round-off errors, but their correlation was not very close.

Obviously, these checks are not significant for the whole working coefficient matrix if some rows or columns of the initial matrix dominate the others, i. e., if the coefficients of one or more rows or columns are much greater than those of the other rows or columns. In this case the checks mainly correspond to the errors of these dominating rows or columns.

The aim of recording these checks was to find out about their usefulness as a trigger for starting a reiteration procedure for eliminating the errors. But their reliability is restricted. Some examples may show that the relation between the checks and the errors did not turn out to be very close. In the figures of group I of the appendix, some of the values of these checks have been plotted. (For the value check = $-\infty$, the value check = -1o has been drawn).

Nevertheless, one may consider to use these checks as a trigger for starting error elimination procedures, e. g., everytime any check reaches the value -5 a reiteration may take place. One point should be mentioned, however. When an "ill-conditioned" vertex is reached, the average error may increase suddenly in this very iteration as the values of the checks may also do. Unfortunately, the error elimination procedures (at least that one used in this investigation) work relatively poorly on "ill-conditioned" vertices. For this reason it might be advantageous to postpone the error elimination until the "ill-conditioned" vertex has been left. In higher dimensional space an "ill-conditioned" junction of hyperplanes with many vertices instead of only one single vertex will occur. In this case the process usually stays at "ill-conditioned" vertices over several iterations, and general, it is difficult to find out whether the "ill-conditioned" junction of hyperplanes has been left or not. Therefore, it might not be too advantageous to use any of these checks as a trigger for immediate error elimination.

In many cases, if the desired precision of the results is not too high, an error elimination will not even be needed. As a matter of fact, the procedure for error elimination takes an extremely long computation time. One reiteration may require more computation time than the whole simplex method.

Another way of eliminating errors is to apply the procedure of equations (11) and (12) only to those columns or rows which seem to have cumulated a particularly high average error. For instance at every $k^{th}$ iteration (k = 1o, 2o, or 5o) the elements of the additional sum row and sum column may be compared to the sums of the current coefficients of the corresponding column or row of the working matrix. If any relative difference reaches a certain threshold this column or row will be cleaned up. Although this has not been tried in this investigation it does not seem to be advisable. As experience shows, the errors of one column or row tend to compensate to a certain extent for the errors of other columns and rows during the iterations. If some columns or rows are cleaned up, this self-compensating process might be disturbed and, therefore, the error cumulation might be accelerated.

Another error elimination procedure on single rows and columns would seem to be advantageous, although no experience can be reported on this particular subject either. This procedure would be to clean up the actual pivot row and pivot column before using them for processing the working matrix according to equation (9). This really seems suitable for keeping the errors of the entire matrix small. However, considerable effort is involved in doing this. For this reason, it might be advisable to make this error elimination dependent on a similar check as outlined in the paragraph above.

## VI. The Zero-Check for Eliminating Non-Significant Elements

During continued matrix operations like the simplex method a lot of small non-significant elements, the actual value of which is zero, usually augment the working coefficient matrix. These elements are caused by round-off errors. They arise in the following manner in a computation of the type:

$$d = a - b \cdot c$$

with e.g. the data (in FORTRAN notation)

$$a = 2 = .20000000 \text{ E } 01$$
$$b = 6 = .60000000 \text{ E } 01$$
$$c = 1/3 = .33333333 \text{ E } 00$$

The results will be:

|  | computed result | precise result |
|---|---|---|
| $b \cdot c =$ | .19999998 E 01 | .20000000 E 01 |
| $d =$ | .20000000 E-06 | .00000000 E 00 |

The absolute values of those non-significant results are not necessarily small if a, b, and c have high values like:

$$a = .20000000 \text{ E } 11$$
$$b = .60000000 \text{ E } 04$$
$$c = .33333333 \text{ E } 07$$

|  | computed result | precise result |
|---|---|---|
| $b \cdot c =$ | .19999998 E 11 | .20000000 E 11 |
| $d =$ | .20000000 E 04 | .00000000 E 00 |

On the other hand, the result d can be a very small number, but is not necessarily non-significant; i.e., need not consist of round-off errors:

$$a = .20000000 \text{ E}-10$$
$$b = .40000000 \text{ E}-02$$
$$c = .51000000 \text{ E}-08$$

```
          computed result        precise result
   b.c =  .20400000 E-1o         .20400000 E-10
   d   =-.40000000 E-12         -.40000000 E-12
```

In the first two cases it will be desirable to set d = 0 while in the third case d should keep its computed value. There are two different ways to carry out a "zero-check" for this purpose, the check with an absolute threshold and the check with a relative threshold.

Several computer programs for the simplex method work with a zero-check that compares the absolute value of each new element after a computation of the type of equation (9) with a threshold $\gamma$ and sets those elements equal to zero, the absolute value of which is smaller than $\gamma$. In FORTRAN this procedure looks like (instead of procedure (1o)):

```
       TEMP = A(I,J) - PC(I)*PR(J)
       IF(ABSF(TEMP)-GAMMA) 101,101,102
   101 TEMP = 0.                                        (18)
   102 A(I,J) = TEMP
```

where GAMMA stands for $\gamma$.

A check of this type does not consume much more computation time than procedure (1o), but it still has several disadvantages:

(1) If the values of the single elements of the matrix vary over a wide range as in the three small examples given in the beginning of this chapter, a very careful scaling has to take place before starting the actual computation. The scaling procedure may have to be repeated after several iterations.

(2) Even after scaling, this zero-check is not very reliable. If the values of the coefficients of the initial matrix only vary between 0.1 and 10, a threshold $\gamma = 10^{-5}$ can easily eliminate significant coefficients when the smaller elements are being processed while, on the other hand, a $\gamma = 10^{-6}$ may leave many non-significant elements in the matrix when the larger elements are being processed.

For these reasons a relative instead of an absolute zero-check was used in this investigation. By this check the values of $a_{ij}^*$ and $a_{ij}$ (see equation (9)) were compared according to:

$$|a^*_{ij}| > \varepsilon |a_{ij}|$$

or

$$|\frac{a^*_{ij}}{a_{ij}}| > \varepsilon$$

as mentioned in Chapter III (Page 7). The FORTRAN statements for this operation look like:

```
      TEMP = A(I,J) - PC(I)*PR(J)
      IF(A(I,J)) 101, 103, 101
  101 IF(ABSF(TEMP/A(I,J))-EPSILO) 102, 102, 103           (19)
  102 TEMP = 0.
  103 A(I,J) = TEMP
```

where EPSILO stands for $\varepsilon$.

This procedure is more time-consuming [+)] than procedure (10) or (18), but it does not have the same disadvantages, at least not to the same extent. As a matter of fact, it is still not satisfactory in every case. If the $\varepsilon$ chosen is too large, there is some probability of cutting off significant coefficients. On the other hand, if big relative errors have cumulated and $\varepsilon$ is small, the larger non-significant elements will remain in the matrix. Nevertheless, this relative check seems to work out much better than the absolute check.

Several runs have been made with $\varepsilon = 10^{-4}$, $\varepsilon = 10^{-5}$, and $\varepsilon = 10^{-6}$. $\varepsilon = 10^{-4}$ seemed to be too large in many cases. In one case, even $\varepsilon = 10^{-5}$ was too large and cut off significant data. On the other hand, $\varepsilon = 10^{-6}$ left many non-significant elements in the matrix in two or three examples. In most cases, however, it turned out that $\varepsilon = 10^{-5}$ and $\varepsilon = 10^{-6}$ worked equally well. (If the mantissa consists of more, say 11, digits a smaller $\varepsilon$, say $\varepsilon = 10^{-8}$ or $\varepsilon = 10^{-9}$, would be recommendable.)

---

+) A special subroutine in the internal programming language of the computer used may accelerate the procedure (19) effectively. E.g., it may be possible simply to compare the exponents of the two elements $a^*_{ij}$ and $a_{ij}$.

Some statistics dealing with the values of the ratios $|\frac{a_{ij}^*}{a_{ij}}|$ on both sides of the check value $\varepsilon$ were computed in each iteration; e.g. the logarithmic means and the logarithmic standard deviations. In addition, the smallest ratios above $\varepsilon$ and the largest ratios below $\varepsilon$ were recorded. These extreme ratios were the most interesting recordings as far as the proper value of $\varepsilon$ is concerned. In the figures of group II (Fig. II-1 to II-7) in the appendix the logarithms of these extreme values on both sides of $\varepsilon$ are shown for some typical runs. (When no element was eliminated by this zero-check in a single iteration a -10 has been plotted.) For some runs these extreme values of both sides stay far away from the crucial $\varepsilon$, so that several different $\varepsilon$'s will do the same job. In other runs the extreme values are spread out all over the whole range, so that it can be assumed that no $\varepsilon$ will fully satisfy the demand not to cut off any significant element nor, at the same time, to leave a non-significant element in the matrix.

Besides the question of selecting the proper $\varepsilon$, three questions have been considered in connection with the advantages of this zero-check:

(1) How does the relative zero-check influence the average and maximal round-off error?

(2) How effectively does the relative zero-check decrease the number of non-zero elements in the working coefficient matrix?

(3) How effectively does the relative zero-check decrease the total number of operations of the type of equation (9) or procedure (19), respectively?

(1): One might suppose that as one effect of the zero-check, the average and maximal round-off errors would be smaller. As a matter of fact, this does not seem to be true. On one hand, the non-significant elements do indeed cause a cumulation of errors. On the other hand, they tend to compensate existing errors. Both effects seem to be about equally strong. Therefore, the zero-check is no real improvement as far as the error cumulation is concerned. This can be checked with some figures of group I (by comparing figures like I-6 and I-7 or I-10 and I-11 concerning the same test problem run with different $\varepsilon$'s). This comparison, obviously, only holds for those problems the opti-

mal solution of which has been reached, both with and without
the zero-check. In some cases, however, a non-significant element was chosen as pivot element in any iteration by which the whole matrix was blown up. These cases will be discussed later.

2): Obviously, the zero-check keeps the number of non-zero elements small. The amount of this reduction depends on the mathematical method and, particularly, on the size of the problem, its structure and its initial density of non-zero elements. The experience from the test problems of this investigation is that the average saving of the maximal number of non-zero elements over all iterations lies in a range between 1o and 2o percent. The average number of non-zero elements will be reduced similarly. The highest reduction was recorded for the normal simplex method. The maximal saving of the maximal number of non-zero elements was 45 percent for test problem 4. The ratios of reduction of the maximal number of non-zero elements for several test problems are given in Table 2. Furthermore, the current number of non-zero elements of all the iterations for several typical runs are plotted in group III of the figures (Fig. III-1 to III-5) of the appendix.

3): Depending upon the decreased number of non-zero elements, the number of operations (of the type of equation (9)) will be decreased by about the square of the reduction of the elements, since both the fullness of the pivot column and the fullness of the pivot row (or of the equivalent vectors in the revised simplex methods) are smaller. The average saving of operations was between 1o and 3o percent. The maximal saving was almost 7o percent (!) in problem 4; i.e., the number of operations was reduced to less than one third. The relative reductions of operations by the zero-check in the several runs of the test problems are given in Table 2.

|  | Program 1 | | Program 2 | | Program 3 | |
|---|---|---|---|---|---|---|
| | Percentage of the maximal number of non-zero elements | Saving of arithm. opns. | Percentage of the maximal number of non-zero elements | Saving of arithm. opns. | Percentage of the maximal number of non-zero elements | Saving of arithm. opns. |
| Problem | | | | | | |
| 1 | 0.0 | 0.0 | 0.0 | 0.0 | 0.0 | 0.0 |
| 2 | 37.0 | 29.0 | 28.5 | 8.1 | - | - |
| 3 | - | - | 5.8 | 11.5 | 6.4 | 19.8 |
| 4 | 45.2 | 69.5 | 14.4 | 2.5 | 38.2 | 66.5 |
| 5 | - | - | - | - | - | - |
| 6 | 31.7 | 37.5 | 6.9 | 6.2 | 8.3 | 11.4 |
| 7 | - | - | - | - | - | - |
| 8 | - | - | - | - | - | - |
| 9 | 0.0 | 0.0 | 0.0 | 0.0 | 0.0 | 0.0 |
| 10 | 15.8 | 25.1 | 19.7 | 15.0 | 16.3 | 20.5 |
| 11 | 5.4 | 20.2 | - | - | 9.9 | 19.7 |
| 12 | 8.0 | 16.0 | - | - | - | - |
| 13 | - | - | - | - | - | - |
| 14 | - | - | - | - | 9.6 | 12.0 |

Table 2: Relative saving of the maximal number of non-zero elements and of the total number of operations achieved by the relative zero-check

For many runs the comparison of Table 2 could not be made. Either a problem was too large for one of the programs, or the run without zero-check did not yield the correct optimal solution after the matrix had been exploded by pivoting on a non-significant element. Finally, some of the comparison runs (particularly for the less interesting problems 12-14) were not carried out. Problems 1 and 9 were not sensitive to the zero-check because of a small number of iterations or a high initial density of non-zero elements.

Actually, the importance of these three effects of the zero-check is of second order. The main trouble caused by the non-significant elements arises when one of them is selected as the pivot element in any iteration. This explodes the whole working coefficient matrix and leads to completely wrong results. This happened relatively frequently, in particular in problem 5, and was the reason for many runs not attaining the optimal solution in cases where no zero-check took place or the value of $\varepsilon$ was too small.

In order to avoid pivoting at a non-significant element, various tests can be inserted for recognizing whether an element chosen as a pivot element is significant or not. A fairly safe check is to compare this element with the product of the average value of the non-zero coefficients of the pivot row and the average value of the non-zero coefficients of the pivot column. If the absolute value of the pivot element is much smaller, for instance, less than $10^{-4}$ times this product the considered pivot element will be dropped.

Another test is to pre-compute SUM3 (see Chapter V), and to drop the considered pivot element if the absolute value of the new SUM3 turns out to be greater than, for instance, $10^6$ times the absolute value of the former SUM3. This test will only fail in case the sum of pivot row coefficients or pivot column coefficients is close to zero (caused by positive and negative elements).

The experience obtained from this investigation is that the three sums (SUM1, SUM2, and SUM3 described in Chapter V) were immediately increased by a large factor when the pivot element was a non-significant coefficient, but their relative differences remained small. However, after some further iterations the sums usually decreased again while their relative differences became larger. A typical sequence of the values of the sums and their relative differences (Check 1,...,Check 4 described in Chapter V) for problem 5 and program 1 ($\varepsilon = 0$) is given in Table 3 where pivoting at a non-significant element occurred in the 18th iteration.

The process was completely out of order in iteration 18, when these sums increased to an absolute value of the factor $10^9$ higher than before. The values of Check1,...,Check4 only indicated this failure after a few more iterations.

When the pivot element in any iteration has been a non-significant element, the coefficients of the working matrix are so spoiled that even reiteration techniques like equations (11) and (12) are not sufficient for clearing the matrix of the errors. The danger of pivoting at such elements will be decreased efficiently by the zero-check. In addition, those kinds of tests outlined in the latter paragraphs will also serve the same purpose. Unfortunately, these tests have not yet been tried in this investigation.

| Itera-tion | SUM1 | SUM2 | SUM3 | Check1 | Check2 | Check3 | Check4 |
|---|---|---|---|---|---|---|---|
| 17 | +.37214934 E 04 | +.37214933 E 04 | +.37214935 E 04 | -7.39 | -7.78 | -7.57 | -7.54 |
| 18 | -.43020586 E 13 | -.43020583 E 13 | -.43020581 E 13 | -7.22 | -7.00 | -6.81 | -7.10 |
| 19 | -.16740491 E 13 | -.16740489 E 13 | -.16740491 E 13 | -6.97 | -7.41 | -7.19 | -7.13 |
| 20 | -.13531677 E 11 | -.13531500 E 11 | -.13531604 E 11 | -4.88 | -5.27 | -4.74 | -5.04 |
| 21 | -.86116953 E 09 | -.86101139 E 09 | -.86109609 E 09 | -3.74 | -4.07 | -3.57 | -3.87 |
| 22 | -.56946444 E 09 | -.56930631 E 09 | -.56940115 E 09 | -3.56 | -3.95 | -3.41 | -3.71 |
| 23 | -.13318400 E 06 | +.24756616 E 05 | -.80182183 E 05 | +0.07 | -0.40 | +0.05 | -0.10 |

Table 3: Sequence of check values after pivoting at a non-significant element

## VII. "Ill-Conditioned" Vertices

The round-off errors tend to increase particularly rapidly after pivoting at "ill-conditioned" vertices. Those vertices where two or more hyperplanes, each representing one constraint, intersect at a very slight angle are considered as "ill-conditioned". An "ill-conditioned" vertex is for instance given by the intersection of the two constraints:

$$3 x_1 + \phantom{.354} x_2 \leq 6$$
$$x_1 + .354 x_2 \leq 2.001$$

The coordinates at this intersection are $x_1 = 1.5$ and $x_2 = 1.5$. As long as the coefficients of this system are not affected by errors, the results (in this example) will have at least five significant digits (for a computer that works with the precision of eight digits). But if the elements have been changed by errors to:

$$3.000001 x_1 + 1.0000002 x_2 \leq 5.999992$$
$$.9999998 x_1 + .3339996 x_2 \leq 2.001003$$

only two or three, or even less, significant digits might remain in some of the computed coefficients.

Since vertices of this kind cause a great deal of trouble from the point of view of error cumulation, it would be desirable to avoid pivoting at them unless they happen to represent the optimal solution; this, however, is rather unlikely, because in this case the objective function must form an even smaller angle with both of the interacting hyperplanes.

As a matter of fact, pivoting at "ill-conditioned" vertices can be avoided by by-passing. This was tried successfully in program 4, which is a modification of program 1 (see page 2). Usually, in the simplex method one moves along an edge of the polyhedron until a vertex is reached where this edge intersects with another hyperplane. In the modified method, after recognizing a vertex as being "ill-conditioned", one keeps going along the same edge until the next intersecting hyperplane is reached. Thus, the next move has to lead back into the feasible area. This technique corresponds with a proposal of Kendall [5] p. 64, which came to the author's attention after these investigations were carried out: "... the program should, as far as possible, provide for methods of circumventing points at which ill-conditioning is encountered, for example, by finding an alternative route of approximation." The technique of by-passing "ill-conditioned" vertices shall be illustrated by the problem shown in figure IV-1 in the appendix. In the usual simplex method one might go along through the vertices 0, 1, 2, and 3, where vertex 3 represents the optimal solution. Vertex 2 is "ill-conditioned". In order to avoid this vertex, one moves along the vertices 0, 1, 5, 3 in the modified method. (Another way of avoiding vertex 2 would be 0, 1, 6, 3, which, however, has not so far been studied in detail).

The arithmetic procedure of doing this by-passing is based upon two insertions in the usual simplex method:

(1) Recognition of an "Ill-Conditioned" Vertex.

The "ill-conditioned" vertices are formed by two (or more) constraints which cut the coordinates relatively close to one another in comparison to their distance from the origin. For example, in figure IV-1, the distance 1-6 is much smaller than 0-1, and 7-8 is much smaller than 0-7. This characteristic is used for recognizing an "ill-conditioned" vertex as follows.

First, in each iteration, after computing the right hand side vector according to:

$$b_i^* = b_i - \frac{b_r a_{is}}{a_{rs}}$$

(which is equivalent to equation (9)), and setting equal to zero those elements $b_i^*$ which fail the zero-check (see Chapter VI), the non-zero $b_i^*$ will be compared with $b_i$. If $b_i^* < \varepsilon' b_i$ with, for example, $\varepsilon' = 10^{-2}$, this row will be marked by the number of the pivot row. This mark means that this very row may intersect the pivot row in a very slight angle. In the example of figure IV-1, the row touching the points 6, 2, 7 is marked when one moves from vertex 0 to vertex 1. (The mark will be removed if in any later iteration this right hand side element increases by about the same factor). If in any iteration the pivot row chosen (e. g. the line 6-2-7) has such a mark on it, the distance between the points which are indicated by the numbers 7 and 8 in figure IV-1 will be computed. If this distance turns out to be smaller than the distance between the points 0 and 7 by about the same factor $\varepsilon'$, vertex 2 will be regarded as being "ill-conditioned".

(2) The Actual By-passing

In this "ill-conditioned" case, another pivot row will be selected according to the usual rule (except that the very row, which would lead to the "ill-conditioned" vertex, is not considered.) After completing the pivot step at this new pivot row, which leads to vertex 5 in figure IV-1, one has to move along the line formed by the points 5, 3, 4 in the next iteration, and stop at vertex 3, if the move in this direction does not increase the value of the objective function, or otherwise go to point 4. In this iteration the slack variable of the constraint represented by the line 1-2-5-8, which defines the pivot column, has to re-enter the basis. The pivot row is either that one which was avoided in the preceding iteration, which leads to vertex 3, or the next further constraint, which leads to vertex 4, depending upon whether the value of the objective function decreases or increases.

In higher dimensional space this modification works similarly. Let the path of the usual simplex method in figure IV-2 go from the origin through the vertices 1, 2, 3, 4, where 4 represents the optimal solution and 3 is an "ill-conditioned" vertex. The modified method begins the same way through 1 and 2, but a mark is set on the constraint which goes through the vertices 3 and 4 after the pivot step at vertex 1. This mark is the trigger for avoiding the "ill-conditioned" vertex 3. Instead of pivoting at this point, the modified method by-passes to 5 and than goes to the optimum at vertex 4.

In figure IV-3, both the usual and modified method take the same path from the origin along vertices 1, 2, 3, 4, where 4 is the optimal point. Indeed, after pivoting at vertex 1, in the modified method one puts a mark on one constraint because of the "ill-conditioned" vertex 6, as one did in figure IV-2. But this mark will vanish after the pivot step at vertex 2, since at vertex 3 the intersection of the two constraints is not "ill-conditioned" any more.

In figure IV-4, the usual method might go from the origin through the vertices 1, 2, 3, 4, to 5, which is the optimal point. The modified method will avoid vertex 3 and move instead to 6, from there to 4 or 7, depending upon whether the value of the objective function decreases or increases, and finally, to 5.

This modified method (program 4) was applied to several small, artificial problems. In many cases it helped to keep the average and maximal relative error smaller by as much as the factor 1oo.

Before inserting this kind of modification in any program for practical use, some more research should be done on choosing a proper value for $\epsilon'$. Furthermore, the case of several neighboring "ill-conditioned" vertices, which is not covered by the modification programmed up to now, should be covered.

## VIII. Some General Remarks

Finally, some remarks dealing with several additional results should be mentioned.

Since the objective function as mentioned above is particularly sensitive to error cumulation, some special attention should be paid to it in order to ensure that the actual optimal solution is found in the last iteration. It seems to be advisable to apply the reiteration procedure at least to the objective function of the optimal solution to make sure that it really represents the optimum.

Particular care is necessary in handling the auxiliary objective function of equation (6), (7). If one of the constraints of which equation (6) is composed dominates the others, or if these constraints sum up to an awkwardly structured equation, it may easily happen that the computation process will terminate within phase 1; i.e., that no feasible solution can be found. This occurred in several test problems. By scaling, i.e., multiplying some of the constraints by a factor of, for example, 1o or 1oo, this kind of failure could be avoided.

One way of handling constraints of the form of equation (8) is to create two equivalent constraints of equation (2) which have the same coefficients, but different signs, such as:

$$\sum_{j=1}^{n} a_{kj} x_j \leq b_k$$

and

$$-\sum_{j=1}^{n} a_{kj} x_j \leq -b_k$$

Due to round-off errors, this will very often lead to a situation in which only one of both constraints can be fulfilled at the same time.

An important topic is the effect of scaling; i. e., multiplying rows or columns by a certain factor. It should be emphasized that scaling (in floating point computation) has no effect at all on operations of the kind which occurs in equation (9). In linear programming procedures, scaling has an influence only on:

(1) The checks mentioned in Chapter V

(2) The absolute zero-check mentioned in Chapter VI, not, however, on the relative zero-check

(3) The selection of the pivot column (depending, however, on the criterion of selecting)

(4) The quality of the auxiliary objective function of equation (6) for phase 1, as mentioned above

Some remarks should be made on the advantages and disadvantages of using double precision operations. Two ways of using double precision are to be distinguished:

(1) <u>Double</u> precision computation and <u>single</u> precision storage

(2) <u>Double</u> precision computation and <u>double</u> precision storage

The general disadvantage of double precision computation is the greater demand of computation time. The disadvantage of double precision storage is that it requires double as much storage space, and storage space is usually the most crucial point in solving linear programming problems. Therefore, double precision storage should be taken into consideration only in special cases.

As far as round-off errors are concerned, double precision computation has the following properties:

(1) It does not prevent non-zero but non-significant elements, which are to be eliminated by means of the zero-check mentioned in Chapter VI. However, the relative values of these elements will usually be much smaller, and therefore, the choice of a proper value of $\varepsilon$ is less crucial.

(2) In most cases, double precision computation will keep the round-off errors small. But in some "ill-conditioned" or nearly "ill-conditioned" cases, which cause the main trouble from the point of view of round-off error cumulation, there will be no improvement through double precision computation (and single precision storage),

as shown in the following example of two successive operations:

$$e = a - b \cdot c$$
$$g = f - d \cdot e$$

with

$a = 2$
$b = 1$
$c = \frac{1126}{1125} = 1.0008888$
$d = 2$
$f = 2$

where e will be stored in single precision. The results (in FORTRAN notation) are:

$e = .99911111 \text{ E } 00$ and
$g = .17777700 \text{ E-}02$ instead of $g = .17777777 \text{ E-}02$

The same loss of two significant digits would be obtained by single or double precision computation.

Thus, in general, double precision computation combined with single precision storage does not seem to be too advantageous. There is no guarantee of getting an improvement sufficiently significant from the point of view of error cumulation to justify the much greater amount of computation time. On the other hand, double precision computation combined with double precision storage will certainly serve the purpose of keeping the errors small; however, the additional effort for storage and access of the intermediate data is usually extremely great.

In the revised simplex method with product form of the inverse the column vectors representing the inverse are of the kind (see [2] pp. 197-2o1, [3] pp. 11o-113):

$$\underline{k} \text{ with } k_i = \begin{cases} \dfrac{a_{is}}{a_{rs}} & \text{for } i \neq r \\ 1 - \dfrac{1}{a_{rs}} & \text{for } i = r \end{cases}$$

In cases, where the pivot element $a_{rs}$ happens to be much greater than 1 the element $k_r$ may cause large errors in the successive iterations for the following reason. For e.g., $a_{rs}$ = 7000, that element will be $k_r$ = .99985714 E 00, where only the last five digits represent the actual $a_{rs}$. Therefore, it acts like a coefficient with five significant digits instead of eight. It is advisable to store only $-\frac{1}{a_{rs}}$ = -.14285714 E-03 instead of $(1 - \frac{1}{a_{rs}})$ and to take care of the constant +1 by modifying the program slightly. This is done in most of the existing computer codes.

It can happen (depending on the code) that round-off errors cause a negative right hand side element instead of zero. For instance, let

$$a_{1s} = 14 \qquad\qquad b_1 = 6.0000001$$
$$a_{rs} = 21 \qquad\qquad b_r = 9.0000001$$

If the element $b_1$ is computed by:

$$b_1^* = b_1 - (\frac{a_{1s}}{a_{rs}}) b_r$$

and the computed fraction is $(\frac{a_{1s}}{a_{rs}})$ = .6666667 the new element will be:

$$b_1^* = 6.0000001 - .6666667 * 9.0000001 = -.00000027,$$

even though $\frac{b_r}{a_{rs}} < \frac{b_1}{a_{1s}}$. These negative elements will be prevented by a modification of the zero-check (see Chapter VI). Even if a linear programming code does not contain the general zero-check, it should contain this check for the right hand side, at least with $\varepsilon$ = 0.

## IX. Acknowledgment

This investigation was made possible by the grant of a one year's NATO Research Fellowship for studying these problems in the United States in 1963/64 and by considerable support from the Operations Research Center of the University of California, Berkeley. The author is particularly grateful to Prof. G. B. Dantzig, the director of the Operations Research Center at that time, from whom he learned many details concerning advanced linear programming which were most valuable for this investigation. Furthermore, many ideas used in this investigation are due to Roy Harvey (Standard Oil Company of California), Saul Gass, and Earl Bell (both at the Operations Research Center at that time), with whom the author enjoyed the opportunity of discussing special questions having to do with this study. The author's interest in investigating round-off error problems in the context of linear programming was initiated by the late Prof. A. Walther (Technische Hochschule Darmstadt, Germany) to whom the author owes particular gratitude.

# Appendix

Group I of the following figures shows how the relative round-off errors increased in several test runs from the first to the last simplex iteration. The single curves have the following meaning:

$M$ = logarithm of the logarithmic mean of the relative errors (equation (15)),

$E_{max}$ = logarithm of the largest relative error (equation (17)),

$S$ = logarithm of the logarithmic standard deviation of the relative errors (equation (16)),

Check1 ... Check5 = Test values related to the errors (See Chapter V).

Group II of the figures refers to the maximal ratios $\left|\frac{a_{ij}^*}{a_{ij}}\right|$ below $\varepsilon$ and the minimal ratios above $\varepsilon$ for several test runs. The logarithms of these ratios are plotted. (See Chapter VI).

The figures of group III show the increase of the number of non-zero elements of the working coefficient matrix, depending upon the value of $\varepsilon$. The results are plotted for $\varepsilon = 0$ (no zero-check) and for $\varepsilon > 0$. (See Chapter VI).

Group IV of the figures serves the purpose of illustrating the modification of the simplex method for avoiding pivoting at "ill-conditioned" vertices. (See Chapter VII).

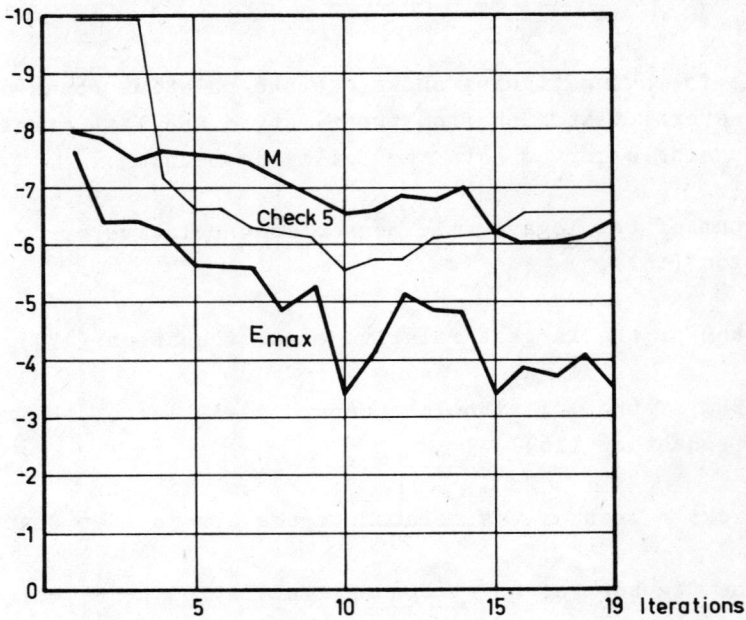

**Fig. I-1:** Problem no. 1o. Program no. 2. $\varepsilon = 10^{-5}$.
No error elimination.

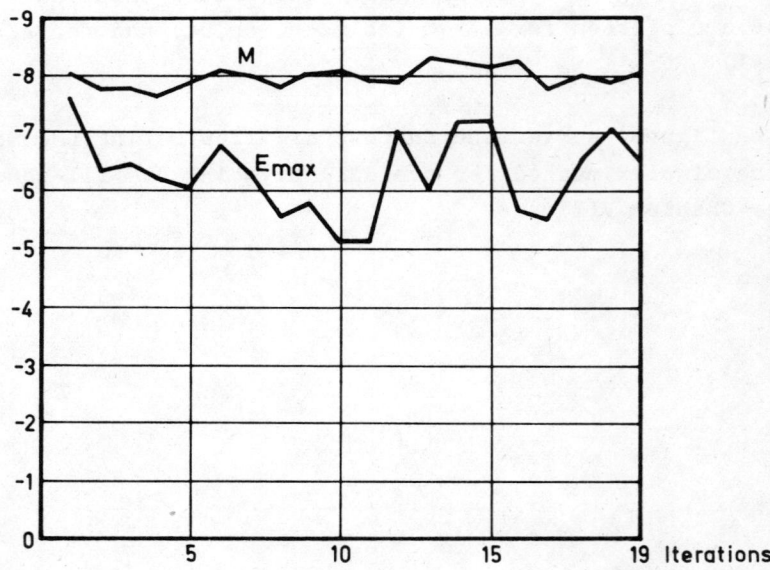

**Fig. I-2:** Problem no. 1o. Program no. 2. $\varepsilon = 10^{-5}$
Error elimination after each iteration.

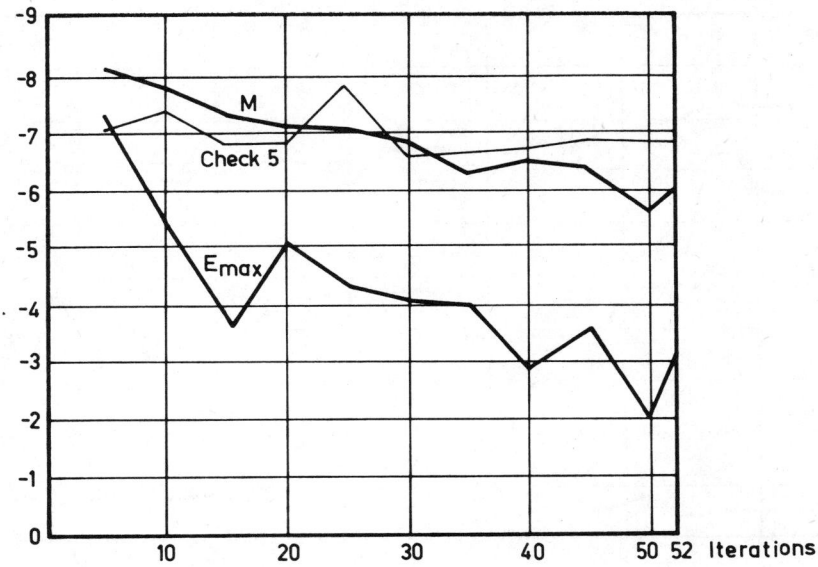

**Fig. I-3:** Problem no. 3. Program no. 2. $\varepsilon = 10^{-5}$.
No error elimination.

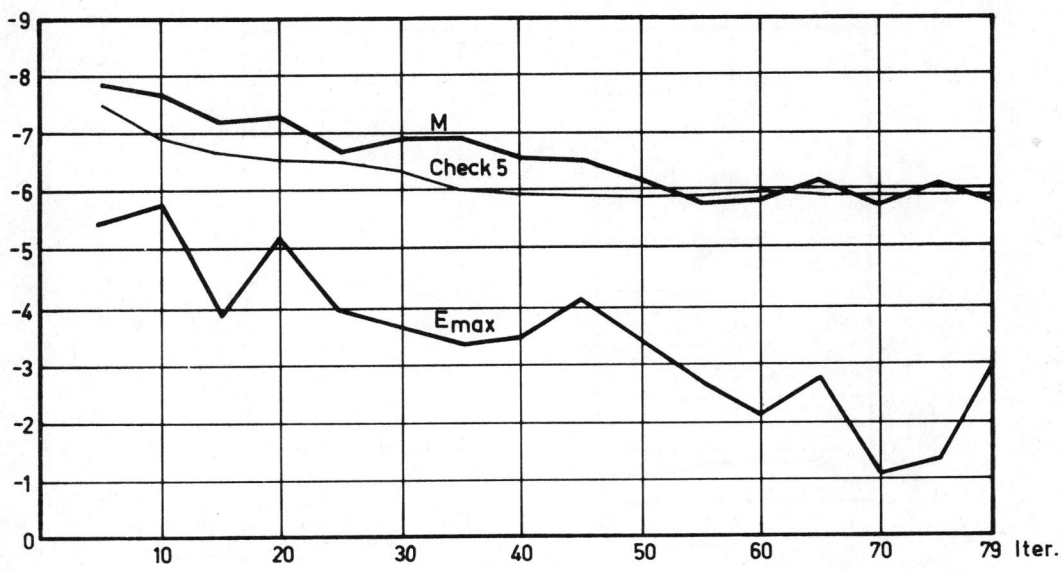

**Fig. I-4:** Problem no. 6. Program no. 2. $\varepsilon = 10^{-6}$. No error elimination.

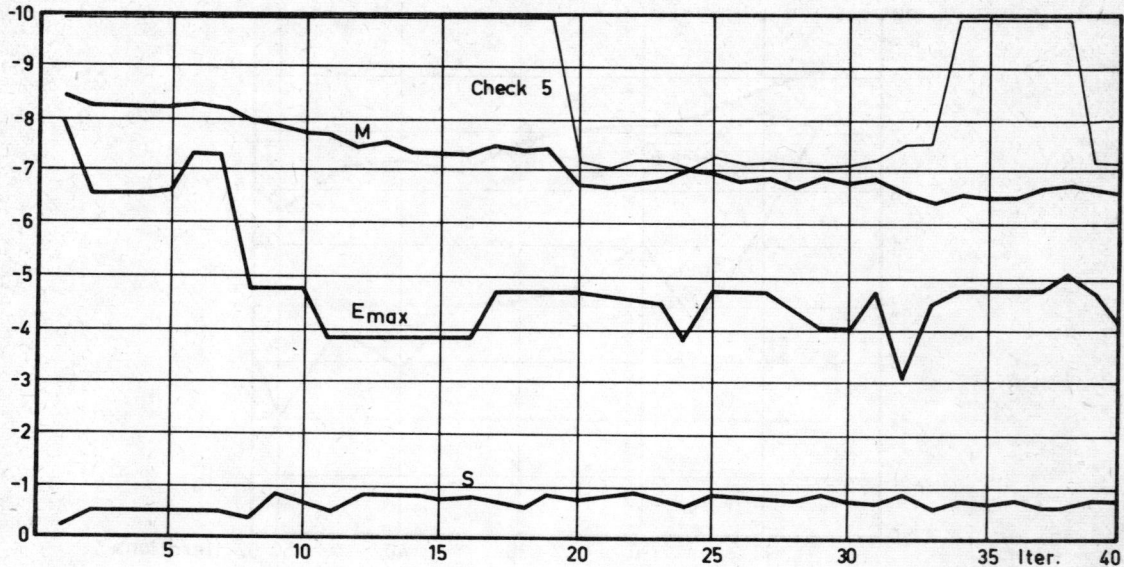

Fig. I-5: Problem no. 5. Program no. 2. $\varepsilon = 10^{-4}$. No error elimination.

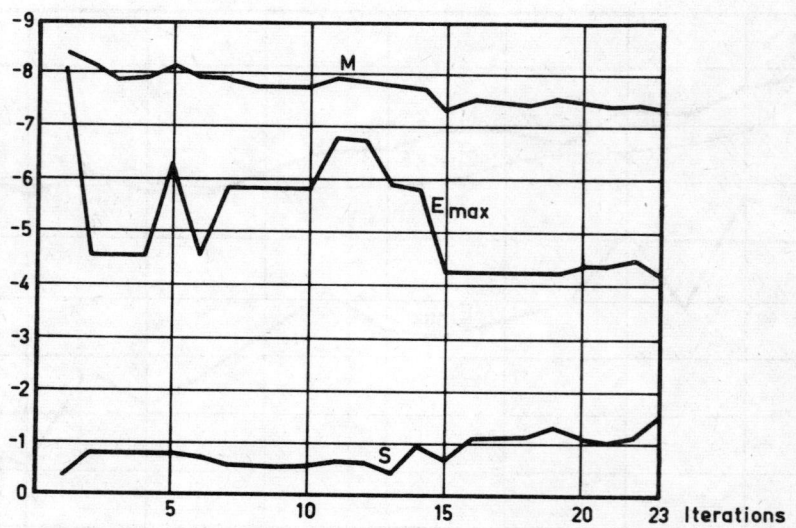

Fig. I-6: Problem no. 4. Program no. 2. $\varepsilon = 0$.
No error elimination.

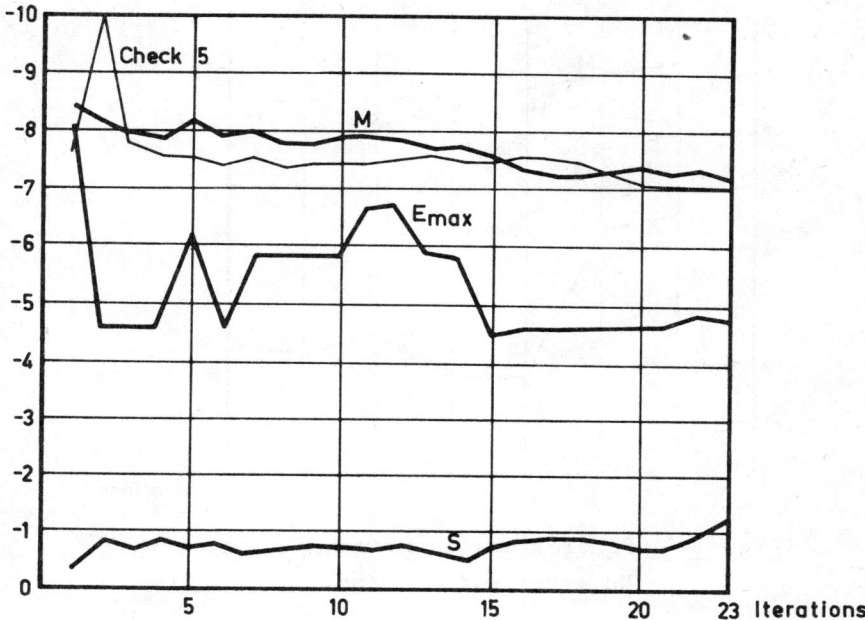

**Fig. I-7:** Problem no. 4. Program no. 2. $\varepsilon = 10^{-4}$.
No error elimination.

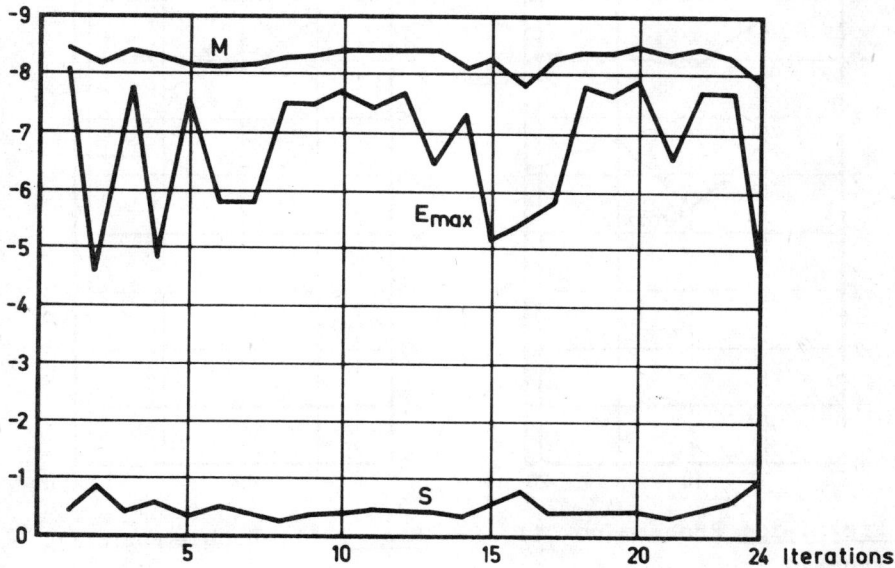

**Fig. I-8:** Problem no. 4. Program no. 2. $\varepsilon = 10^{-4}$.
Error elimination after each iteration.

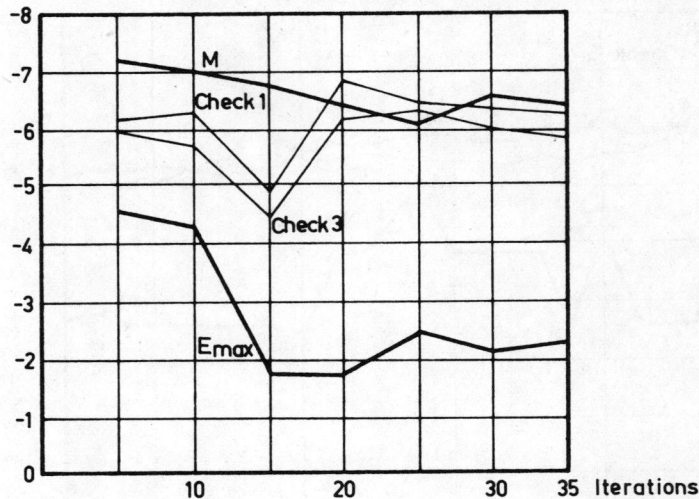

**Fig. I-9:** Problem no. 8. Program no. 1. $\varepsilon = 10^{-6}$.
No error elimination.

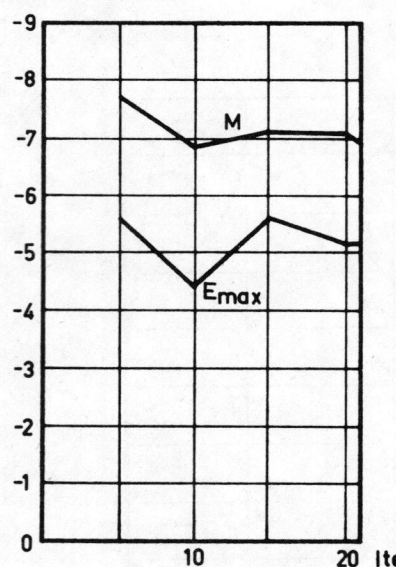

**Fig. I-10:** Problem no. 11.
Program no. 1. $\varepsilon = 0$.
No error elimination.

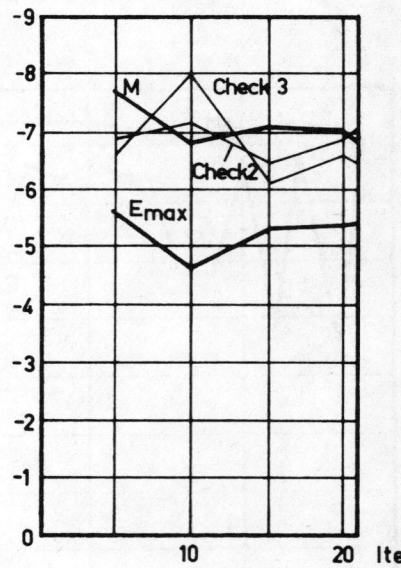

**Fig. I-11:** Problem no. 11.
Program no. 1. $\varepsilon = 10^{-5}$.
No error elimination.

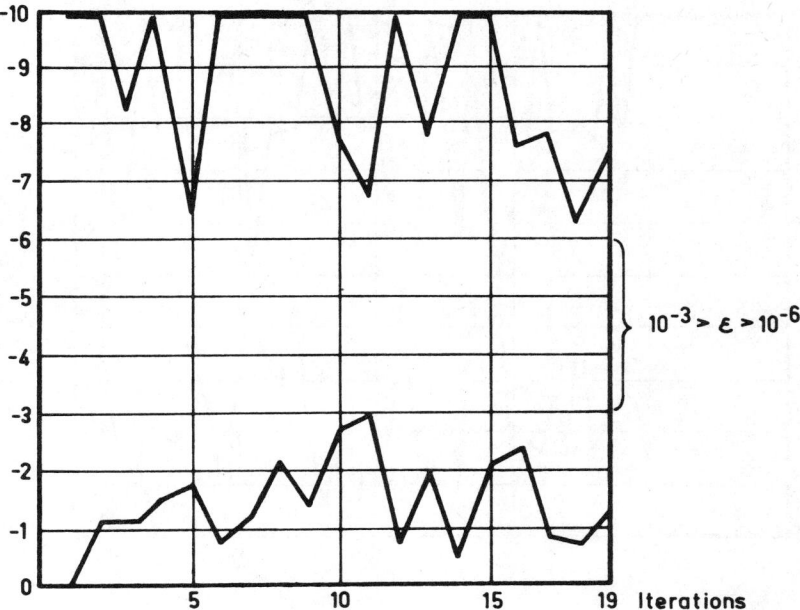

**Fig. II-1:** Problem no. 1o. Program no. 2.
No error elimination.

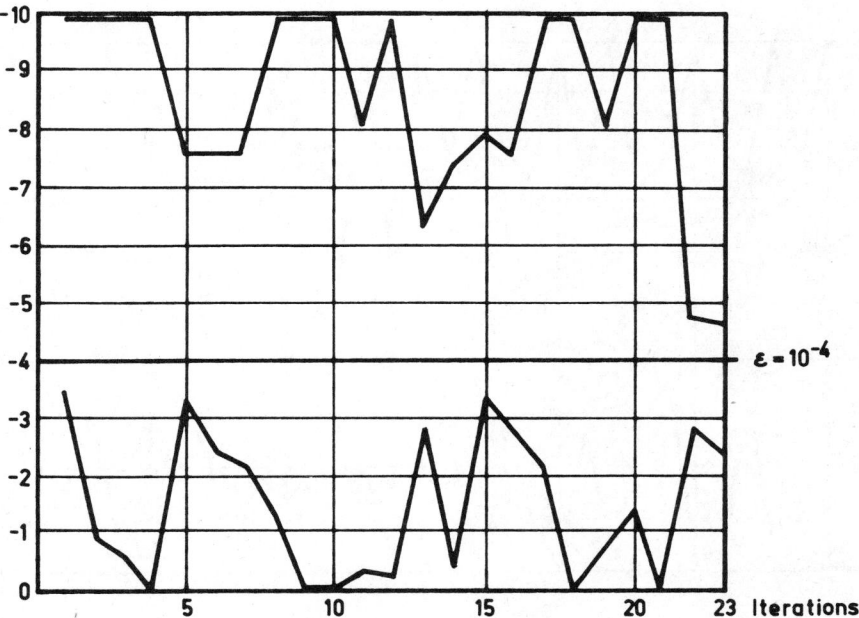

**Fig. II-2:** Problem no. 4. Program no. 2.
No error elimination.

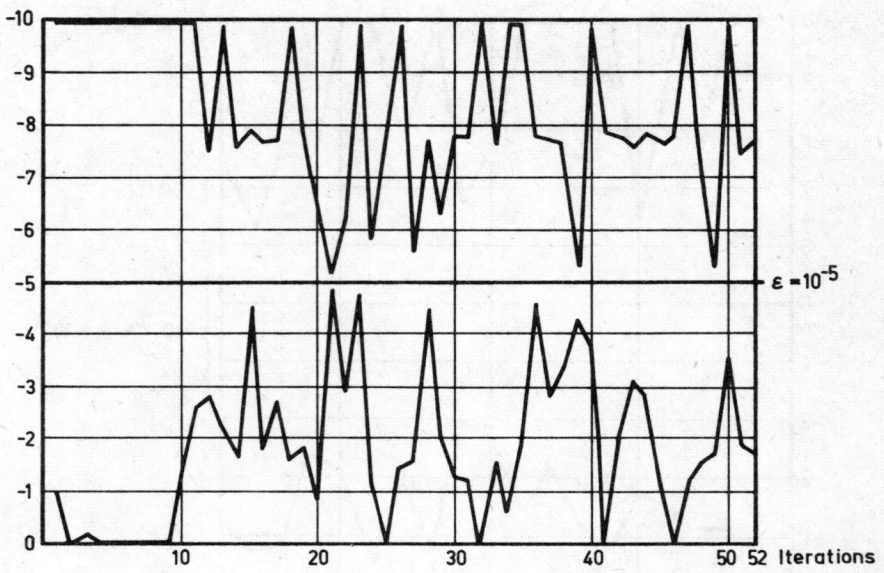

Fig. II-3: Problem no. 3. Program no. 2.
No error elimination.

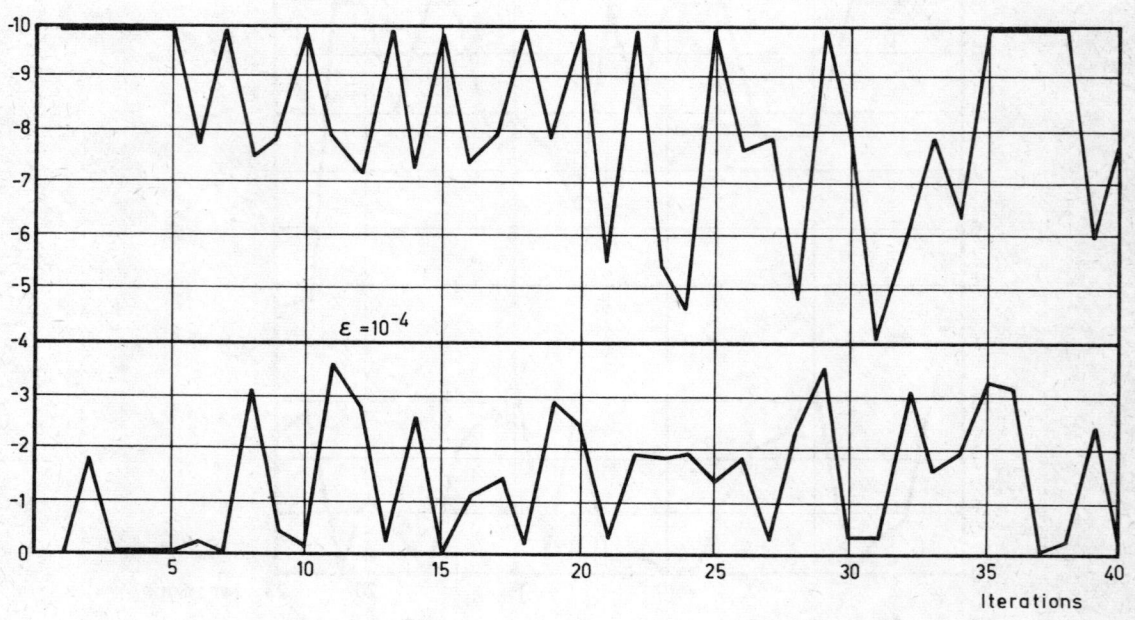

Fig. II-4: Problem no. 5. Program no. 2.
No error elimination.

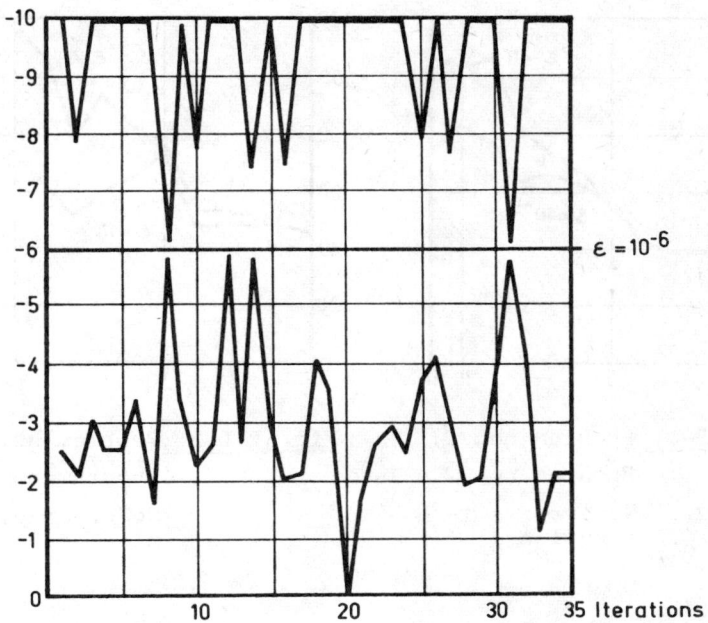

Fig. II-5: Problem no. 8. Program no. 1.
No error elimination.

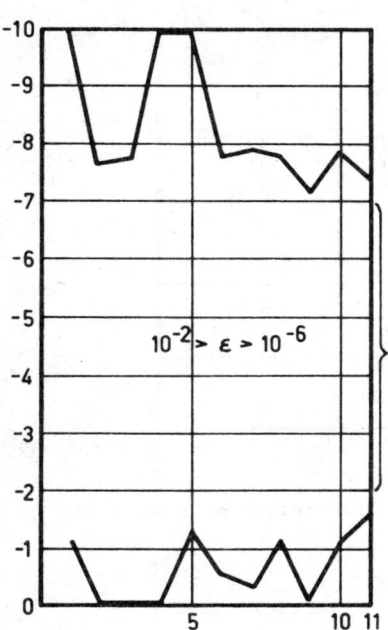

Fig. II-6: Problem no. 2.
Program no. 2.
No error elimination.

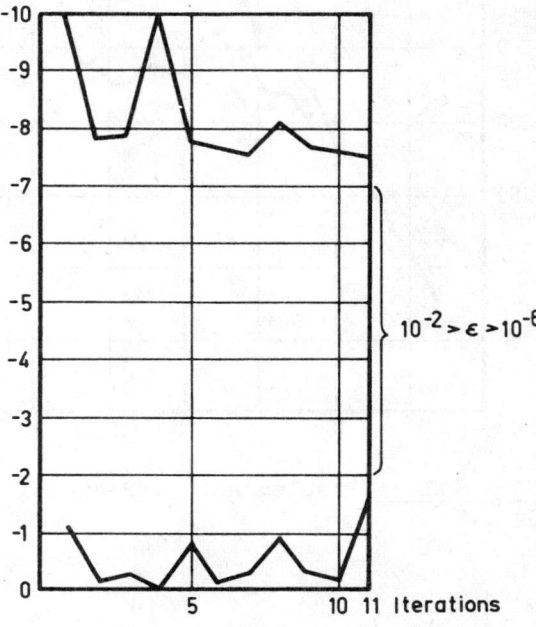

Fig. II-7: Problem no. 2.
Program no. 2.
No error elimination.

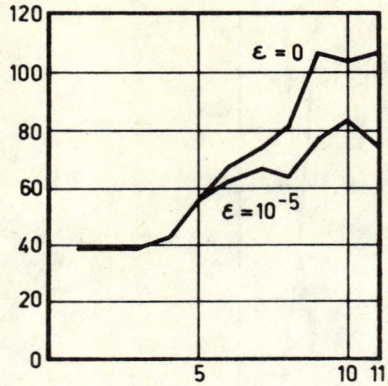 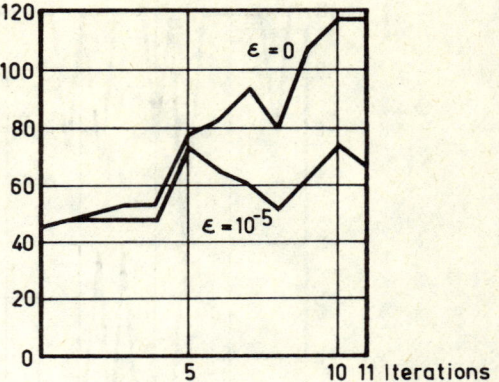

Fig. III-1: Problem no. 2. Program no. 2. No error elimination.

Fig. III-2: Problem no. 2. Program no. 1. No error elimination.

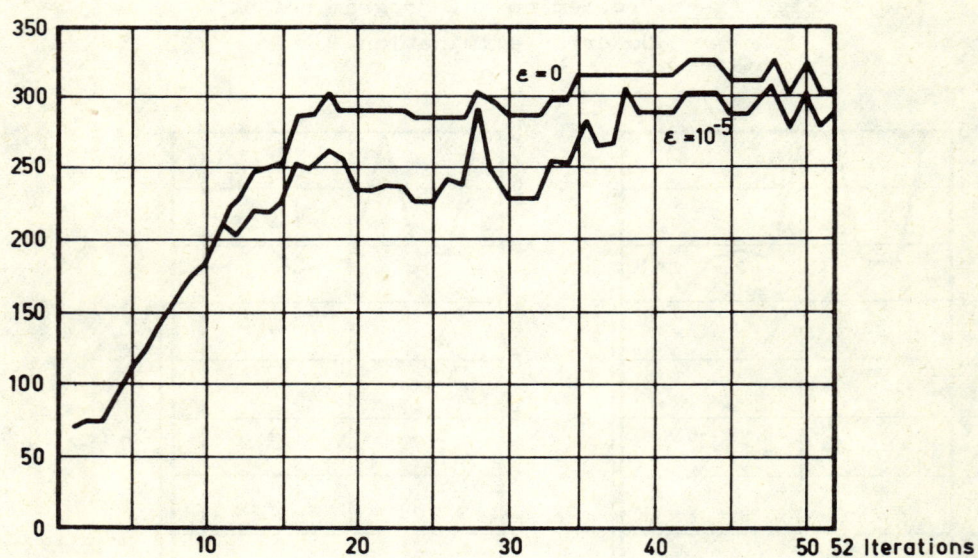

Fig. III-3: Problem no. 3. Program no. 2. No error elimination.

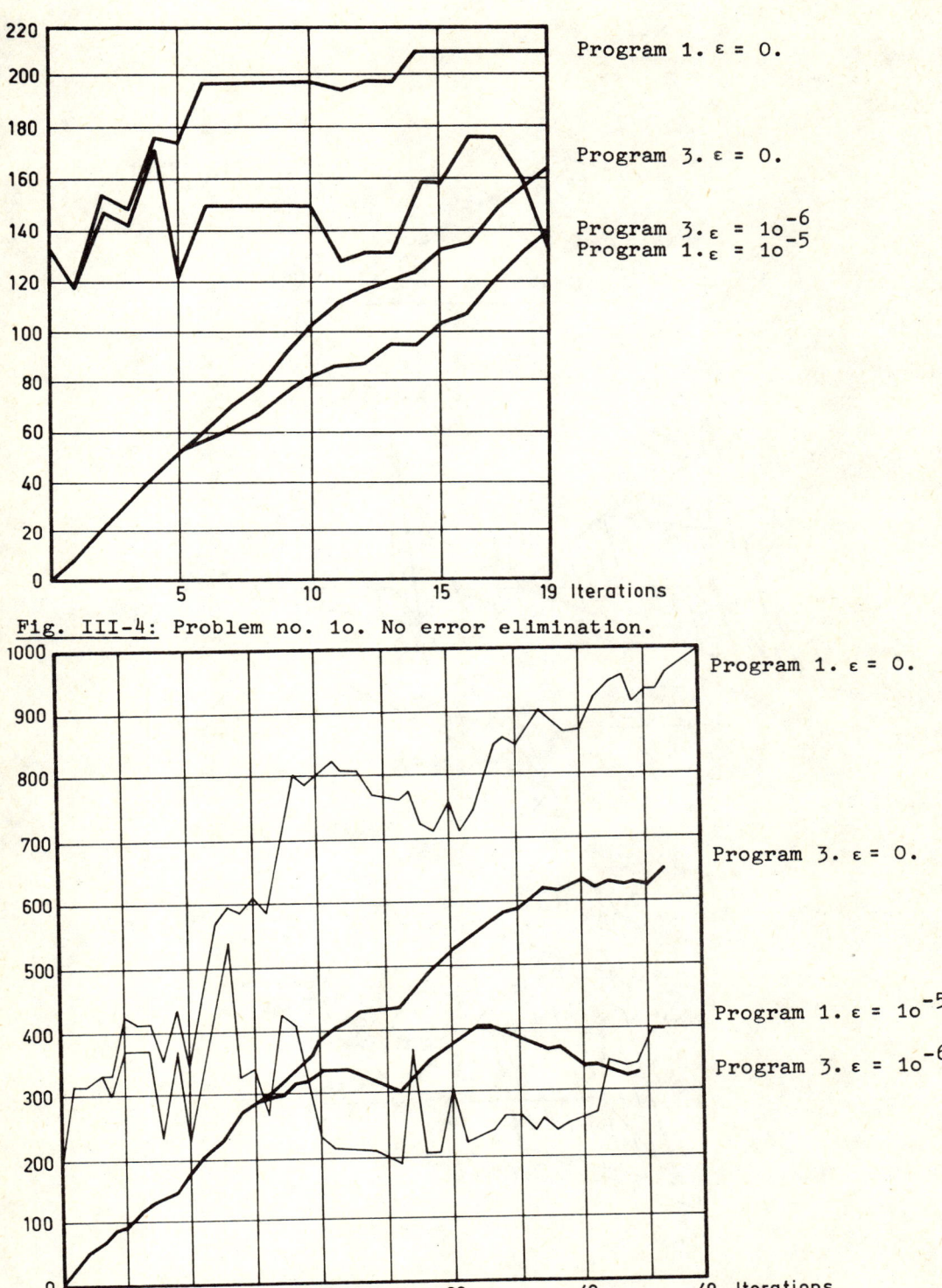

Fig. III-4: Problem no. 1o. No error elimination.

Fig. III-5: Problem no. 4. No error elimination.

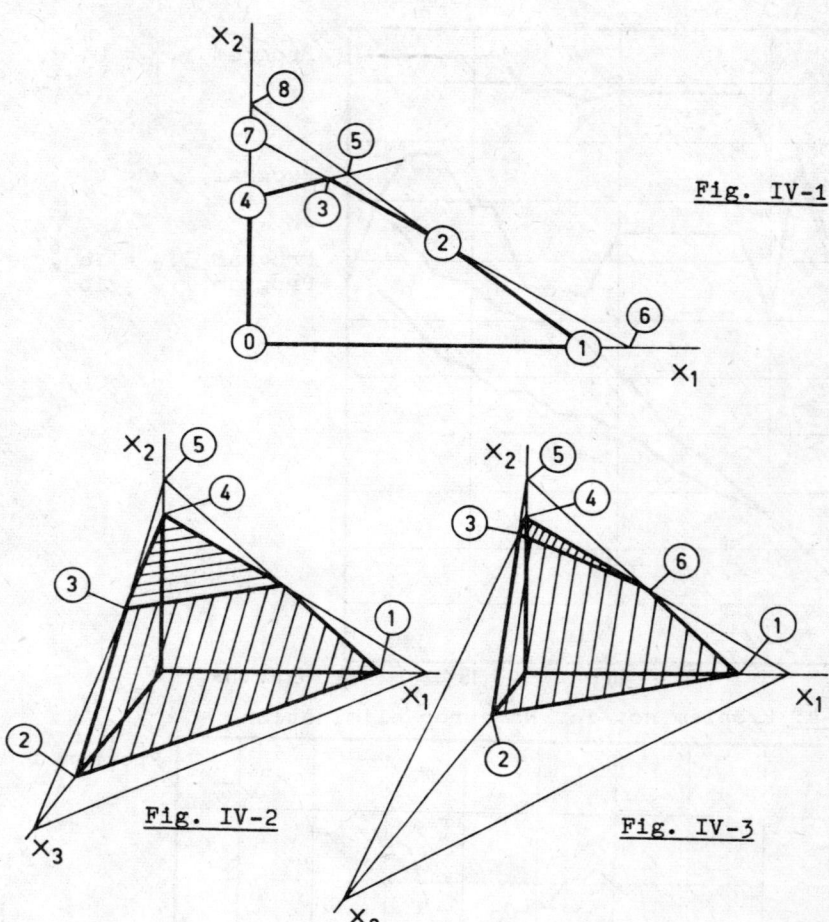

Fig. IV-1

Fig. IV-2

Fig. IV-3

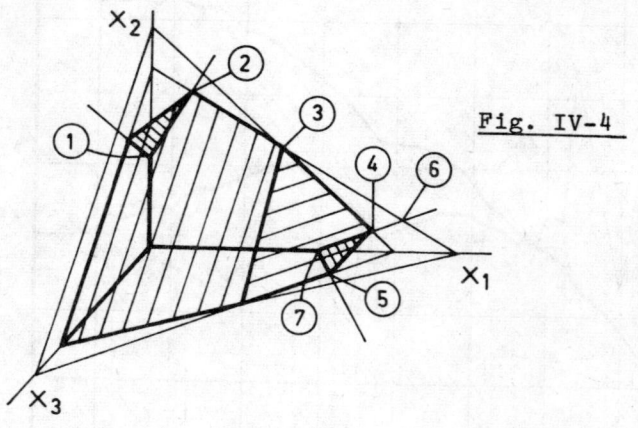

Fig. IV-4

References

[1] Cutler, Leola, Philip Wolfe: Experiments in Linear Programming. In [4], pp. 177-200.

[2] Dantzig, George B.: Linear Programming and Extensions. Princeton, New Jersey, 1963.

[3] Gass, Saul I.: Linear Programming: Methods and Applications. 2. Edition, New York, 1964.

[4] Graves, Robert L., Philip Wolfe (Editors): Recent Advances in Mathematical Programming. New York, 1963.

[5] Kendall, M. G.: Ill-Conditioned Matrices in Linear Programming. Metrika, Vol. 6 (1963), pp. 60-64.

[6] Müller-Merbach, Heiner: Die symmetrische revidierte Simplex-Methode der linearen Planungsrechnung. Elektronische Datenverarbeitung, Vol. 7 (1965), No. 3, pp. 105-113.

[7] Müller-Merbach, Heiner: Operations Research. Berlin, Frankfurt/M., 1969.

[8] Rall, Louis B. (Editor): Error in Digital Computation, Vol. 1. New York, 1964.

[9] Rall, Louis B. (Editor): Error in Digital Computation, Vol. 2. New York, 1965.

[10] Stiefel, Eduard: Einführung in die numerische Mathematik. 2. Aufl., Stuttgart, 1963.

[11] Wilkinson, J. H.: Error Analysis of Direct Methods of Matrix Inversion. Journal ACM, Vol. 8 (1961), No. 3, pp. 281-330.

[12] Wilkinson, J. H.: Error Analysis of Floating-Point Computation. Numerische Mathematik, Vol. 2 (1960), pp. 319-340.

[13] Wilkinson, J. H.: Rounding Errors in Algebraic Processes. London, 1963.

[14] Wolfe, Philip: **Error in the Solution of Linear Programming Problems.** In [8], pp. 271-284.

[15] Zurmühl, Rudolf: **Praktische Mathematik für Ingenieure und Mathematiker.** 4. Aufl., Berlin, 1963.

# Lecture Notes in Operations Research and Mathematical Systems

Vol. 1: H. Bühlmann, H. Loeffel, E. Nievergelt, Einführung in die Theorie und Praxis der Entscheidung bei Unsicherheit. 2. Auflage, IV, 125 Seiten 4°. 1969. DM 12,− / US $ 3.30

Vol. 2: U. N. Bhat, A Study of the Queueing Systems M/G/1 and GI/M/1. VIII, 78 pages. 4°. 1968. DM 8,80 / US $ 2.50

Vol. 3: A. Strauss, An Introduction to Optimal Control Theory. VI, 153 pages. 4°. 1968. DM 14,− / US $ 3.90

Vol. 4: Einführung in die Methode Branch and Bound. Herausgegeben von F. Weinberg. VIII, 159 Seiten. 4°. 1968. DM 14,− / US $ 3.90

Vol. 5: L. Hyvärinen, Information Theory for Systems Engineers. VIII, 205 pages. 4°. 1968. DM 15,20 / US $ 4.20

Vol. 6: H. P. Künzi, O. Müller, E. Nievergelt, Einführungskursus in die dynamische Programmierung. IV, 103 Seiten. 4°. 1968. DM 9,− / US $ 2.50

Vol. 7: W. Popp, Einführung in die Theorie der Lagerhaltung. VI, 173 Seiten. 4°. 1968. DM 14,80 / US $ 4.10

Vol. 8: J. Teghem, J. Loris-Teghem, J. P. Lambotte, Modèles d'Attente M/G/1 et GI/M/1 à Arrivées et Services en Groupes. IV, 53 pages. 4°. 1969. DM 6,− / US $ 1.70

Vol. 9: E. Schultze, Einführung in die mathematischen Grundlagen der Informationstheorie. VI, 116 Seiten. 4°. 1969. DM 10,− / US $ 2.80

Vol. 10: D. Hochstädter, Stochastische Lagerhaltungsmodelle. VI, 269 Seiten. 4°. 1969. DM 18,− / US $ 5.00

Vol. 11/12: Mathematical Systems Theory and Economics. Edited by H. W. Kuhn and G. P. Szegö. VIII, IV, 486 pages. 4°. 1969. DM 34,− / US $ 9.40

Vol. 13: Heuristische Planungsmethoden. Herausgegeben von F. Weinberg und C. A. Zehnder. II, 93 Seiten. 4°. 1969. DM 8,− / US $ 2.20

Vol. 14: Computing Methods in Optimization Problems. Edited by A. V. Balakrishnan. V, 191 pages. 4°. 1969. DM 14,− / US $ 3.90

Vol. 15: Economic Models, Estimation and Risk Programming: Essays in Honor of Gerhard Tintner. Edited by K. A. Fox, G. V. L. Narasimham and J. K. Sengupta. VIII, 461 pages. 4°. 1969. DM 24,− / US $ 6.60

Vol. 16: H. P. Künzi und W. Oettli, Nichtlineare Optimierung: Neuere Verfahren, Bibliographie. IV, 180 Seiten. 4°. 1969. DM 12,− / US $ 3.30

Vol. 17: H. Bauer und K. Neumann, Berechnung optimaler Steuerungen, Maximumprinzip und dynamische Optimierung. VIII, 188 Seiten. 4°. 1969. DM 14,− / US $ 3.90

Vol. 18: M. Wolff, Optimale Instandhaltungspolitiken in einfachen Systemen. V, 143 Seiten. 4°. 1970. DM 12,− / US $ 3.30

Vol. 19: L. Hyvärinen, Mathematical Modeling for Industrial Processes. VI, 122 pages. 4°. 1970. DM 10,− / US $ 2.80

Vol. 20: G. Uebe, Optimale Fahrpläne. IX, 161 Seiten. 4°. 1970. DM 12,− / US $ 3.30

Vol. 21: Th. Liebling, Graphentheorie in Planungs- und Tourenproblemen am Beispiel des städtischen Straßendienstes. IX, 118 Seiten. 4°. 1970. DM 12,− / US $ 3.30

Vol. 22: W. Eichhorn, Theorie der homogenen Produktionsfunktion. VIII, 119 Seiten. 4°. 1970. DM 12,− / US $ 3.30

Vol. 23: A. Ghosal, Some Aspects of Queueing and Storage Systems. IV, 93 pages. 4°. 1970. DM 10,− / US $ 2.80

RAYMOND H. LIBRARY

Vol. 24: Feichtinger, Lernprozesse in stochastischen Automaten.
V, 66 Seiten. 4°. 1970. DM 6,– / $ 1.70

Vol. 25: R. Henn und O. Opitz, Konsum- und Produktionstheorie I.
II, 124 Seiten. 4°. 1970. DM 10,– / $ 2.80

Vol. 26: D. Hochstädter und G. Uebe, Ökonometrische Methoden.
XII, 250 Seit

Vol. 27: I. H
IV, 45 page

Vol. 28: The                                            by R. B. Banerji and
M. D. Mesa

Vol. 29: S.
III, 177 page

Vol. 30: H.                                       ungsproblemen.
VI, 102 Seit

Vol. 31: M.
II, 106 Seite

Vol. 32: F. E                                      nearer Sprachen.
XII, 143 Seit

Vol. 33: K. H                                      ith Discrete Time Parameter.
VI, 160 page

Vol. 34: H. S                                     heorie und Anwendungen.
VII, 128 Seit

Vol. 35: F. F

Vol. 36: M.
VI, 95 pages

Vol. 37: H. M
VI, 48 page

T
57.74
M84
1970

JUL 23 1974